This book belongs to:

_____

Thank you and God bless

Orf.

The Blissful Forest (The Fruits of the Spirit)
Copyright© 2024 by David Oyewole
Contact: oyewoledavid70@yahoo.com

Acknowledgement

I will like to acknowledge my wife; Venelia Oyewole. My children; David Oyewole Jr, Joel Oyewole, and Eden Oyewole for supporting me throughout this journey.

Hi! My name is Wisdom, Welcome to the Blissful Forest.
I live here and I am known throughout the forest for my SELF CONTROL and great advice.

SELF CONTROL is being able to control our thoughts, desires, words, and actions to make the right decisions. With Wisdom comes SELF CONTROL.

One day, a rabbit was hopping joyfully in the forest and hopped past Wisdom. Her name was JOY.
Joy was full of fun.

Hey there, my name is Wisdom, what's your name?

Wisdom saw how happy JOY was and asked if they could be friends. Joy happily agreed.

Together, they went on a journey across the forest to spread their Joy and wisdom with new friends.

Hello Wisdom, I AM JOY!!!

On their journey, Wisdom and Joy met a Deer named GOOD.
Good knew right from wrong and would always make the right choices. He was made the judge of the forest for being truthful.

Good decided to join them as they went on to spread Wisdom, Joy, and Goodness across the forest and to make new friends.

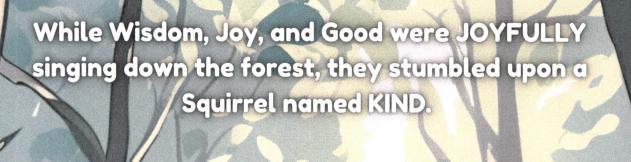

While Wisdom, Joy, and Good were JOYFULLY singing down the forest, they stumbled upon a Squirrel named KIND.

Kind was known in the forest for always lending a helping hand and sharing her things with others.

Wisdom, Joy, and Good saw Kind carrying out an act of kindness by sharing her food. They asked Kind to join them in spreading Wisdom, Joy, goodness, and kindness across the forest and make new friends.
Kind agreed and they went on their merry way.

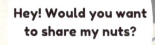

Hey! Would you want to share my nuts?

Yes PLEASE! Thank you for sharing.

The four friends got to the river and decided it was time to rest. While they were resting, they met a turtle named PATIENCE.

While talking to Patience, Joy said 'I just can't wait for the whole forest to experience us! The Joy, Goodness, Wisdom, and Kindness. I JUST CAN'T WAIT!'

Patience replied saying 'Joy! I can see how excited you are for the forest to feel your presence. But I say to you, do not stop, keep going and in time, with patience, your wish will come true.

I will not give up and I will be patient

Keep going!

Thank you for your advice Patience.

'Come with us' asked Wisdom,
'I will be glad to' replied Patience.

Further down in the forest, Wisdom, Joy, Good, Kind, and Patience came across twin doves; PEACE and GENTLE.

Hello, I am Gentle and my sister is Peace.

The presence of Gentle and Peace brought the forest in harmony and CALM

Wisdom, Joy, Good, Kind, and Patience felt so safe and welcomed in the presence of Peace and Gentle.

Hello up there, my name is Patience.

'Would you like to join us on our quest to make the forest a better place' asked Kind to Peace and Gentle,
'YES WE WILL' answered Peace.

At the edge of the forest by the stream, the company of friends gathered to celebrate completing their quest of sharing Wisdom, Joy, Goodness, Kindness, Patience, Peace, Gentleness and Faithfulness across the forest.

Then came a Swan called LOVE.

Love has it all...

Love is PATIENT and KIND, Love does not show off to make her friends feel bad, she is not rude. She does not make you do only what she wants, she is not grumpy and she does not like unkindness but is happy with the truth.

with LOVE, WISDOM, JOY, PATIENCE, PEACE, GOODNESS, KINDNESS, GENTLENESS, and FAITHFULNESS, there was Bliss in the forest.

The next pages are for you to write something about the different Fruits of the Spirit in your own words

Self Control

Joy

Goodness

_____

_____

_____

_____

_____

_____

_____

_____

_____

_____

_____

_____

Kindness

_____

_____

_____

_____

_____

_____

_____

_____

_____

_____

_____

Patience

Gentleness

Peace

Faithfulness

Love